Reading Photographs

Reading Photographs
Understanding the Aesthetics of Photography

The Photographers' Gallery

BY JONATHAN BAYER

with essays by
Ainslie Ellis, Ian Jeffrey
and Peter Turner

Pantheon Books, New York

Library of Congress Cataloguing in Publication Data
Photographers' Gallery.
Reading Photographs.
Originally published under title: Concerning Photography.
Originally published as the catalogue of an exhibition held at The Photographers' Gallery, London, and Spectro Workshop, Newcastle upon Tyne, in 1977.
    1. Photography, Artistic. 2. Photography, Artistic—Exhibitions.
I. Spectro Workshop. II. Title.
TR183.P47 1978   770'.1   77-88761
ISBN 0-394-50127-6

ISBN 0-394-73584-6 pbk.

Manufactured in the United States of America

Designed by Denis Piper and Mike Kenny
987654

Acknowledgements

We would like to express our thanks to all those people who have given us help with the collection and acquisition of the photographs we needed for the exhibition.

Firstly to those who have loaned from personal or institutional collections. Jonathan Bayer; Rosellina Bischof Burri, Kunsthaus, Zürich; Peter Castle, Victoria and Albert Museum; Martin Heiferman, Castelli Graphics; Ralph Gibson; Ian Jeffrey; Paul Joyce; Paul Hill; Barry Lane, Arts Council of Great Britain; Julien Levy; Chris Steele-Perkins; Peter Turner. We would also like to thank all the photographers who kindly lent their own work. Secondly all those who have very kindly loaned us work on consignment over a considerable period. Russ Anderson; Paul Katz, Marlborough Gallery, New York; Barbara Lloyd, Marlborough Graphics, London; Harry Lunn, Graphics International, Washington D.C.

Thirdly to all those who gave us their time and advice. Terence LeGoubin, Colorific; Martin Heiferman, Castelli Graphics; John Hillelson, Magnum Photos, London; Joan Liftin, Magnum Photos, New York; Si Lowinsky, Phoenix Gallery, San Francisco; Victor Schrager, Light Gallery, New York; Lee Witkin, New York; JoAnne Verburg, George Eastman House.

We would also like to thank everyone who worked closely with us in the production of the exhibition and the catalogue. Bryn Campbell for editing the catalogue and Heather Forbes for her work on the index. Denis Piper and Mike Kenny for the Design and also Mike Treasure and Andy Ganf for inspiration and initial research.

Finally we are especially grateful to The Olympus Optical Company and Kodak Limited for their very timely financial donations which helped us enormously to acquire the bulk of the photographs in the exhibition.

Contents

Foreword. Sue Davies

This book originated as a catalogue for an exhibition organised by The Photographers' Gallery, London, in 1977, and it is presented here with only minor alterations. Our primary object was to help people to a better understanding of contemporary photography by describing some of the major considerations that have been common throughout the history of the medium and illustrating them with examples from the last seventy years. Clearly, it would have been impossible to cover all areas of photography, and so we decided to use the urban landscape as a basis for the specific points we wished to make. This produced the required cohesion, but it must be remembered that many of the particular things said about light, time and composition in this context could apply equally to landscape, portraiture or any other form of creative photography.

Although the idea of producing a somewhat didactic exhibition about the aesthetics of photography came from the Gallery, this book is chiefly the work of Jonathan Bayer. He did most of the initial research and wrote the introductions to each section. He was also largely responsible for the final selection of prints. Keeping a balance between familiar and new images was a formidable job and one for which he deserves much praise.

Bayer's introductions have been augmented by essays not specifically concerned with the exhibition but showing some of the ways in which people deeply involved with photography look at and enjoy photographs. We would like to thank Ainslie Ellis, Peter Turner and Ian Jeffrey for undertaking this assignment.

We would also like to thank the photographers, most of whom have not been shown in mixed exhibitions for many years. They have allowed us to select from their work those pictures we felt made our points most clearly, rather than ones they themselves may have preferred, and have generally shown a trust in our judgement for which we are truly grateful.

We hope that this book will help people enjoy and appreciate photography more than they may do already. Showing how various photographers, over the years, have explored or reacted against certain creative possibilities of the medium may help to explain something of what is happening in photography today. We know that these images are 'good photographs,' and we ask only that you look at them with fresh eyes and in relation to those around them, even when some may be very familiar to you. In short, our aim is to broaden the understanding of photography in the most enjoyable way possible.

Introduction: Awareness and the photographer. Ainslie Ellis

Early on in that remarkable novel *Ragtime* by E. L. Doctorow there is a reference to Freud's visit to America to give a series of lectures at Clark University in Massachusetts. And Chapter 5 of Part One ends like this:

"Of course Freud's immediate reception in America was not auspicious. A few professional alienists understood his importance, but to most of the public he appeared as some kind of German sexologist, an exponent of free love who used big words to talk about dirty things. At least a decade would have to pass before Freud would have his revenge and see his ideas begin to destroy sex in America forever."

By that stage in the novel we are already hooked on Doctorow's images, his taut energy, his narrative power. But, if I am not completely mistaken, when we read the last sentence of the passage I have quoted, we are engaged in a new way. A challenge has been issued and our tidy or untidy attic of beliefs and assumptions about love, sex, Freud or whatever, is about to be rummaged in. We are, I suspect, surprised for a moment but, in the same instant, welcome the idea. Our twentieth-century mass beliefs are so often assumed and interpreted for us by the media, or by scientists, specialists, pundits and politicians who all tell us what we think, why we think it and why it is important (to them) that we should think something else. You are not asked to think for yourself. You are supplied with a panel of prepared answers from which you are invited to choose. That is something wholly different.

Before attempting to write an introduction to this catalogue I became, once again, aware of the danger of putting forward, in however personal and fallible a fashion, any ideas I may have on how one may approach photography in order to understand it.

Whatever one says about so sensitive, important and complex a matter is liable to be misunderstood, misquoted, or hacked out of context on some future occasion. You cannot understand life, you can only live it. In the living grows the understanding. Doing English Literature will not help you to love — therefore to understand — poetry. It may well help you in textual analysis and further your academic prospects, an entirely different kettle of fish. And the way to have some grasp, some love, some real enjoyment of, say, music is to expose yourself to as much of it as possible; to perform, take part, or listen with your whole attention.

Now that last word contains the great secret. If we can bring to a piece of music, or to a photograph, our whole attention, then, and then only, something remarkable *can* happen. We are open. Something can be said between the listener, or the person looking, and the work in hand. The most dangerous thing is to come to an exhibition full of —

well, I won't call them prejudices, but well-formulated opinions of the kind of photograph you like, the feeling it should give you, or the social message it should convey. This will effectively turn off, or divert, the nature of your attention. Attention is creative, as Simone Weil remarked, and attention is what any good, let alone great, photographer deserves. And nothing more?

Something more, indeed. A knowledge, swiftly and easily acquired today from illustrated photographic histories and exhibitions, of the broad sweep of that part of the visual highway occupied by the images of great photographers. Many can be found in this exhibition gathered under a loose but useful classification of approach. If I appear to be making the understanding of a photograph too simplistic, to merely equal attention plus a grasp of its visual history, I am doing this deliberately. Art? Photography is one medium, like architecture, painting, ceramics, within the whole. Not more, nor less than this. Aesthetics? Too often the pot-boilings of critics or academics rather than creators. Semiotics? An attempt to force visual imagery into the jargon of linguistics and so become subject to merely political and social interpretations. It is, of course, possible to force photography into either Joseph's coat or a strait-jacket. But none of this helps.

Photography is concerned with images which are the product of light and awareness. Light is the essential key in a process that uses optical, mechanical and chemical means to form a permanent image. But awareness of the photographer alone illuminates and vivifies this process. To what subjects, in what way, he *applies* his openness is now the marrow and the matter of our concern.

No doubt I shall be accused of obscurantism or elitism, or have some other ill-merited label attached, if I write here that I am convinced that the nature of awareness is concerned on the one hand, with what the Greeks called *aretê,* or excellence. On the other hand, it is at one with a quality of tension that can, by its very nature, elicit what Cartier-Bresson has called 'the decisive moment'. At the same instant, or overseeing both, is a quality of relaxed attention, something most difficult to achieve and almost impossible to turn on at will. All of these three, awareness in the sense of *aretê,* tension in Cartier-Bresson's and Herrigel's sense (in *Zen in the Art of Archery*) and attention in Simone Weil's, mean that we are talking in short of discipline. An onerous word, but one heavy with creative capability. A word which, for the wrong reasons derided, or perhaps for the right ones in the wrong context, *has* to return. Without it, we are rudderless.

Yes, we are speaking of images. Of the creation of images by photographic means. Words can only serve as clues to the why and how, or to some of the why and some of the how, of creating potent and creative photographs.

Some of the clues lie buried in Pirsig's *Zen and the Art of Motorcycle Maintenance* which ought to be compulsory reading for anyone ambitious, or foolish, enough to teach not merely photography but creative photography to boot. Pirsig quotes in this book a passage from H. D. F. Kitto's *The Greeks.* Kitto writes: 'When we meet *aretê* in Plato, we translate it "virtue" and consequently miss all the flavour of it.'

' "Virtue", at least in modern English, is almost entirely a moral word; *aretê,* on the other hand, is used indifferently in all the categories, and simply means excellence.' He goes on to point out that the hero of the Odyssey is in fact an excellent all-rounder who has surpassing *aretê.*

'*Aretê* implies a respect for the wholeness or oneness of life, and a consequent dislike of specialization. It implies a contempt for efficiency — or rather a much higher idea of efficiency, an efficiency which exists not in one department of life but in life itself.'

Eighteen months or so ago I wrote in *The British Journal of Photography* a piece which ended with the assertion that I would write no more on the subject of photography. But when I read and hear, everywhere, that photography has become (infected by the contagion of "art"?) so commercially self-conscious that we are even concerned how much so-and-so can sell his prints for, with values, therefore, that are no longer matters of quality, of inward excellence, but are largely related to the starting-prices in the market, it is surely time to bring into question, to re-examine, the real and inherent values, the true quality of a good photograph. To learn how these may be recognised. And how, if at all, any of these factors ought to concern future photographers and therefore how photography is taught.

I do not believe for an instant, that we should leave all this to connoisseurs, to specialists, to critics, or to dealers. They will have their reward in any event, or a sufficient slice of it. What we need, above everything else, is an informed and interested public that is aware of the scope and nature of photography and consequently cares to go and see the best examples. This exhibition attempts to provide just such an opportunity to review categories of good contemporary work.

If, as I happen to believe, attention, *aretê* and a tension that springs ultimately from self-discipline, are the essentials in the making of a good photograph, how much of this can be self-acquired? How much needs to be taught, or even indicated?

Let me end with a quotation from Eugen Herrigel's little paperback, *Zen in the Art of Archery,* to which Cartier-Bresson has acknowledged his debt.

" 'I' m afraid I don't understand anything more at all,' I answered, 'even the simplest things have got in a muddle. Is it "I" who draws the bow, or is it the bow which draws me into the state of highest tension? Do "I" hit the goal, or does the goal hit me? Is "It" spiritual when seen by the eyes of the body and corporeal when seen by the eyes of the spirit — or both or neither? Bow, arrow, goal and ego, all melt into one another, so that I can no longer separate them. And even the need to separate has gone. For as soon as I take the bow and shoot, everything becomes so clear and straightforward and so ridiculously simple . . .'

'Now at last', the Master broke in, 'the bowstring has cut right through you.' "

Concerning Photography. Jonathan Bayer

"... The process of analysing the effect of a poem ... must be one of impossible complexity — it is true no explanation can be adequate, but ... any one valid reason that can be found is worth giving." William Empson, *Seven Types of Ambiguity.*

This show is an attempt to provide a basic working vocabulary for reading photographs. Photographs that have interested viewers over the years and new images that have more than cursorily challenged contemporary audiences have, in some way, demanded to be read in order to be understood and appreciated. The suggested vocabulary is one of adumbrating the mysteries and ambiguities which, in the course of looking at photographs, involves the viewer in an act of responding to them.

What does one look for in photographs and why do we look at certain photographs more than others? Why are some boring while others transcend the cursory glance to become an aesthetic object? Most photographs communicate the information they contain almost too immediately. They are universally understood, are high in 'human interest' and require little or no further explication. Many are seen every day in newspapers and magazines. We glance at them quickly and turn the page. We have been told the story (most likely with the help of a caption) but the image itself need never be looked at again. However, the challenge is to venture among photographs that are more difficult to understand, images that enter the realm of art because they invite the viewer to participate and to decipher them. These stimulate the mind, assault it, amuse it, set problems for it and give it the sublime satisfaction of coming up with its own answers. "Good" photographic images intrigue, present a mystery, or demand to be read. They are constructs of frustrations and ambiguities which force the viewer to actively interact with the photograph.

To start with a rather simplistic formulation as a basis for aesthetics: the brain, the senses, operate functionally on a level of habit — expectations based on past experience — and only become aware and active in response to stimuli denoting change in their environment. Art operates on an assumption that there is a known framework, an artistic form, vocabulary and syntax that is widely accepted and generally known to others. Changes are made in this framework, expectations are set up and frustrated, the mind is awakened and stimulated. It not only has to react, it has to cope with the problem to resolve it. Thus, the viewer is led into the role of a creator himself. He enters into a dialogue with the image before him, in that he discovers, argues, formulates his own ideas from his own experience and, in general, operates to come to terms with the tensions aroused.

For example, the music of Bach or Mozart can at first glance be readily identified as part of a formula or style. In fact, much genre music is predictable and as a result often uninteresting. However, these composers, while working within the genre, change it, do something unexpected. A fugue starts. The listener expects the progression of the idea in other instruments but the composer proceeds to give the convention a new twist. You are prevented from too readily following the cadence or tune you would like to follow, in short, frustrating your expectations and giving a small fillip of surprise and joy. Nonetheless, the composer comes back to give the listener reassurance, for he is not out merely to destroy but also to re-create experience. He affirms the wholeness of the work not only by resolution but by making the listener actively aware anew of the component parts.

A photograph is capable of such creative stimulus with the vocabulary and within the structure of photography. To understand when the form is being violated and why, one has to study the form. Certainly one should become acquainted with the photographs of the past and the traditions of photography, as many of today's photographs are consciously or unconsciously alluding to these traditions (at times, sadly, merely for the amusement of other photographers). This vocabulary can be set forth so that more people can learn to consciously recognise, to re-see many things to which hitherto they had only an automatic response, things that by quiet assimilation have become part of everyday culture or conventional wisdom.

After looking at a number of photographs it is apparent that the field is enormous and that the categories they can be placed into are endless. Whether landscape, portrait, colour, monochrome . . . each category will have its own peculiar vocabulary with which to become familiar. Convenience and expediency, given the time and availability of photographs, have dictated that the show be pared down to a small, rather arbitrarily limited area, with the hope, nevertheless, that the tools used for approaching a small sample will still be of use for understanding the larger entity.

The show concentrates on photographs of the 20th century, particularly those in some way connected with the urban environment. They are all 'straight' photographs, unmanipulated by such means as montage, solarization, double exposure, etc. On the whole the photographs have a high aesthetic content or are of more than average interest, but the selection has not been made with any intent of being a compendium of landmark photographs nor a definitive history of 20th century photography. The photographs have been chosen primarily for their didactic appropriateness. They have been placed into a category to illustrate a point, though more often than not they could fit into any of a number of other categories. In fact, many people might decide that a photograph fits better in a different category and one object of the show is to set forth a vocabulary so as to allow the viewer the mental excercise of making cross-connections between the categories for himself. The viewer should also creatively confront some of the less familiar photographs and explore whether they are more readily understandable given the vocabulary.

Neither has the show been designed to be an exhaustive catalogue of how to look at photographs nor a definitive syntax of the aesthetics of photography. Such an exercise would be like trying to sweep clear the sand from a beach, an endless task and if successfully done would destroy the viewer's enjoyment in discovering for himself some of the numerous byways of, and enormous variety in, exploring photography. The categories are meant as but signposts to help the viewer orient himself if he finds himself in strange territory, but once engaged, looking feeds upon looking and the mysteries take over to induce the eye to travel over the photographs again and again.

Time

Time embodies one of the basic properties of photography, the ability to capture a fleeting instant, a discrete slice of ongoing action. As in other arts, photography is dependent on the materials it uses. The recording of light is a fundamental property of the film and the print and time is a function of controlling that light. Time and light are not merely tools of the trade but important areas of concern for the photographer.

One way to start reading a picture can be to look at how the artist uses his materials. If one were to say that a painting is "about" paint being applied to a surface, one would proceed to examine what kind of paint is used and how it is applied and make evaluations as to the quality and effect it has on the total image. Similarly one can start looking at photography by saying that it is about time and explore how many ways "time" is important to the photograph.

Photographers have become fascinated with time, both with the means to convey a sense of time as well as with the subject of time itself, as an abstract, philosophical concept. How does time fascinate the viewer? Partly it presents a reality in a way the mind doesn't ordinarily perceive it. Accustomed as it is to coping unconsciously, with an endless flow of sensory perceptions, it stops to examine more closely something it feels it must have seen but never has, such as a motion frozen into a still image. The classic illustration of this is that until Eadweard Muybridge photographed a galloping horse no one had "seen" whether all four of its hooves were airborne at the same time and, if so, in what position they were.

In the days of the heavy, large-format camera which required a long time to set up and long times to expose the negative, images tended to be static, occasionally marked by blurred images of something moving while the camera shutter was open.

Although taken with a relatively large camera, a picture such as Stieglitz' *The Terminal* transcends the limitations of the heavy, unwieldy camera to capture with a feeling of spontaneity a unique moment that is full of immediacy and movement. Stieglitz often called his photographs of this time, 'snapshots', and this photograph is one of the earliest to catch the peak of an everyday, unposed action.

The advent of the light, eminently portable 35mm camera enabled photographs to be taken faster, almost anywhere. The ability to capture a fleeting instant of ordinary everyday life has generically become known as the "decisive moment", a term coined by the arch-practitioner of this type of photography, Henri Cartier-Bresson. In his work the term not only connotes the capturing of the peak of an action but also the moment when all elements are organised to make a balanced, well-composed picture, giving the event its proper expression. In *Behind St. Lazare (page 15)* not only does the viewer linger to wonder what will happen next but he is amazed that the photographer was able to capture the instant at all. The amazement grows as the eye notices the echoes and balances throughout the rest of the picture — the leaping ballet dancer on the poster mirroring the man's leap into space, the shape of the dancer's arched back matched by the hoops in the water, the moving rhythms of the fixed fence contrasted with the frozen action of the moving man. Even the hands of the clock seem poised in sympathy with the angle of the man's leap.

Similarly, Sorgi's *Suicide (page 18)* rivets the eye. It has become more than a run-of-the-mill news picture. Time is conveyed almost as in a comic strip. In one frame, the unaware, unconcerned people in the coffee shop, as if no event were taking place. In another frame, the doorway of the hotel, the policeman 'handles the situation' about to happen. Outside, the un-handled event itself happening and, lastly, in the mind's eye, the imagined dénouement. There is the ironic touch of the sign, "Give Till It Hurts . . ." Not least we feel the tension between the bizarrely beautiful form of the falling body, the ordinariness of the hotel and the certain ugliness and horror of the moment to come.

Time is often portrayed by deliberately using blurred movement, an inheritance from the accidents of large-format photography. Coolly as in Steinert's *Pedestrian (page 16)* where the durability of the pattern of the grid and bricks is stressed by the fleetingness of the pedestrian who, like the Cheshire cat, is in the process of mysteriously vanishing. Or, with more immediacy and impressionism, as in William Klein's picture of children in New York *(page 17)*. It can also be done iconographically, as in Atget's fair scene *(page 14)*. Here the clock seems to announce that the picture is about time. Atget has magically conveyed, despite, or because of, the complete stillness of the image, that in a few moments the panels of the stage will open and the show will commence, that this is only an interlude in the bustle of the fair. The viewer must wait and in the meantime explore the décor and detail before him and keep his eye on the time. Yet the clock is not a real one, just a facsimile with hands that can be moved to show the time of the next show; time is just a man-made convention. And the stage is a richly painted façade, in contrast with the shabby but real, bare boards. Suddenly the mind is given a picture rich with allusions, rich with nostalgia, sadness, a sense of time past and time lost —

"Life's but a walking shadow, a poor player
That struts and frets his hour upon the stage
And then is heard no more . . . ." *Macbeth*

9 Eugène Atget

2 Henri Cartier-Bresson

7 Otto Steinert

16

8 William Klein

3 I. Russell Sorgi

5 Paul Trevor

Symbol

A good photograph can evoke infinite associations from the viewer's own experience, other photographs and even the other arts. The symbol concentrates this function and creates new awareness. It is the result of the conscious or unconscious act of the photographer to imbue a detail, a gesture, or a scene with a more universal meaning. With penetrating insight he sees into the scene before him and by use of the appropriate symbol arouses a corresponding intuition in others. It gathers force as continual evocation makes it familiar and as each iteration evokes all accumulated connotations.

The range of use of symbolism is wide. At one end of the spectrum a photograph presents an ordinary object or situation in such a way as to imply an enhanced meaning based on mutual knowledge about that object. At the other end of the spectrum the viewer can be given a less specific scene, an 'equivalent' such as a picture of just clouds, where he is invited to free-associate, investigate his own emotions freed from the photographer's personal lexicon of meanings.

Stieglitz's *The Hand of Man* is of the first category, making associations with industrialization, the power of the steam engine and even with the scientism of impressionist painting (viz. Monet's painting *Gare St. Lazare*). The title suggests a rather laudatory, admiring view of man's achievements and the picture itself seems to present a romantic beauty about steam and railways.

Similarly, the pistol on the lazily insolent, cocked hip of the policeman in Shahn's, *On duty during strike; Morgantown, West Virginia,* alludes to a common fund of attitudes about 'law and order', policemen, or the gun as power in U.S. society (sheathed but flaunted). One feels one knows exactly how the strikers might fare at this man's hands, though there is no evidence of the strike itself in the picture.

Robert Frank's *Bar (page 23)* raises the juke box to the level of a cult, if not a religious, idol, with its light emanating like a holy aura, a symbol of the bizarre ecstasy of roadhouse culture. (In his book, *The Americans,* Frank amplified this theme, building up the image of the jukebox through repeated use of pictures in which it featured). In fact, one can look at the number of Frank photographs elsewhere in the show and observe not only his keen awareness of American culture but also note how his personal vocabulary, like Walker Evans' in the 1930's, has become a symbol for a whole era.

New symbols are continually being created. Winogrand's *San Marcos, Texas (page 25)*, readily implies a larger meaningfulness in the paper cups, the snack baskets and the plastic chairs of the drive-in restaurant. With the scotch-taped signs on the window, the blank backs of ads for whipped ersatz ice-cream, the scene condenses into a microcosm the urban-suburban-interurban, sleek but tatty drive-in culture. On the other hand the question is quite open whether by merely pointing out a strange detail, Bernard Deschamps has succeeded in being as richly evocative.

Certain images have become meaningful by becoming familiar. The automobile has been a favourite object which either photographers have used to comment on society or the viewer has naturally read as being such a comment. Paul Strand's *Automobile Wheel,* focused closely on the car, a detail that conveys the beauty of the machine. Walker Evans' *Joe's Auto Graveyard* places the sad corpses of the machines wasted by man into the stark natural beauty of the land. And both Cartier-Bresson and Art Sinsabaugh show in different ways how man is dominated or herded by the automobile culture. It would seem that in the course of the century, photography has drifted away from finding and preserving beauty in the thing itself, to contrasting with increasingly bitter irony the surface beauty with a more tragic reality, or ignoring the façade completely, showing banality and ugliness 'as it is'. Either this is a shift from involvement to alienation, or a renewed attempt to become aware of, and involved with, the "ordinary" — that which is usually an object of contempt.

The sign, the billboard, the written word photographed has also been a favourite conceit of photographers. Brassai's *Graffitti* celebrates the plasticity and texture of the found object. But such photographs more commonly rely on the humour or irony of the contrast between the words and their environment. Occasionally such pictures can touch a deeper pathos, such as Evans' *Torn Movie Poster.* A most beautiful and powerfully composed picture, it becomes an allegory on the decay of the glamour of the public image, with the more durable base material re-emerging through the veneer.

More obviously humorous is the match between Carol Lombard's eyes and the architecture of the buildings in Evans' "Love Before Breakfast" billboard.

In Margaret Bourke-White's picture, the simple irony of the breadline in front of the sign reading "world's highest standard of living", though blunt photojournalism, does not detract from the rhythms of the picture and the peoples' faces. Nathan Lyons adds pictorial wit to his picture by the way he places the sign in relation to the picture's edge.

Walker Evans' *Corrugated Tin Façade (page 26)* no doubt shocked when it first appeared; 'Why show us an ordinary, dilapidated tin shack?' Indeed it is 'hideous' and ordinary but, with contemplation and exploration it reveals depths of beauty. First its tremendous clarity and sharpness and the sheer tactility of the light glancing across the corrugated surface, then the interplay of rectangular shapes, framed pictures within the picture; the rectangle of the building itself and its rhythm of tin panels, the doors large and small, and the mysterious floating rectangle the eye creates of the five panels and sign under the centrally raised portion of the façade. The sharp lines of the top of the building also make the sky itself another panel of flatness. The picture reduces to a marvelous array of interlocking shapes so that it is transformed from an object of disintegration into an abstract integration. It is with continuing scrutiny that things at first overlooked, emerge with enhanced importance. Lewis Baltz' corrugated concrete wall *(page 27)* speaking to a more sophisticated generation of viewers, needs fewer clues around the edges to place the object in time and environment. In fact the further removal of clues arouses the interest and curiosity of the spectator while at the same time going a step further in abstracting the object and concentrating on the qualities and rhythms of light and the texture of the wall. Still, enough detail remains to evoke the vast emptiness of a large industrial estate.

13 Robert Frank

19 Clarence John Laughlin

14 Garry Winogrand

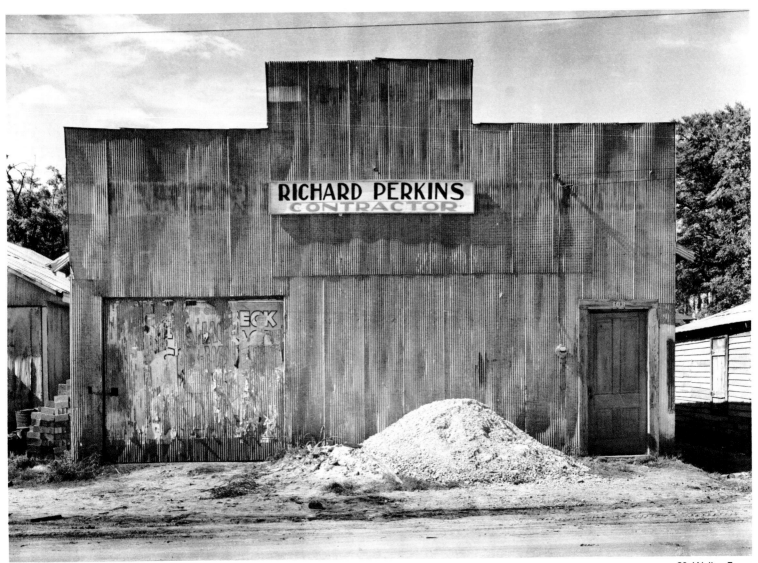

29 Walker Evans

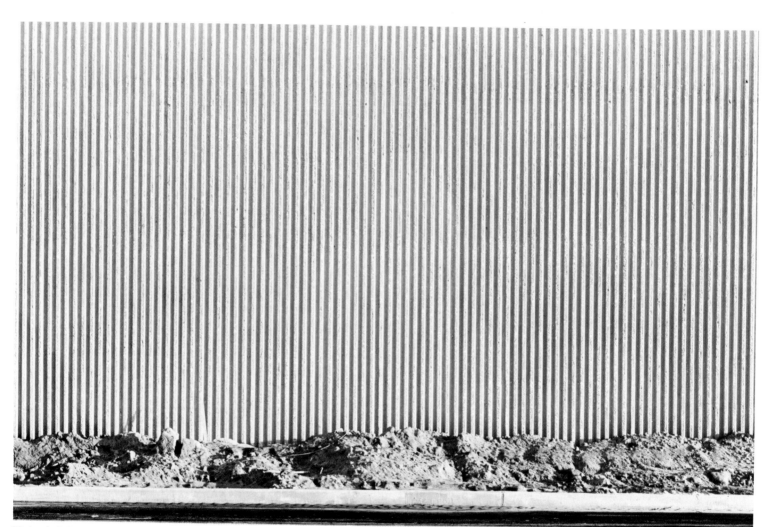

30 Lewis Baltz

Organization of the Picture

Numerous ways can be used to organize a photograph. Unlike the painter, the photographer has greater difficulty in building up the organization of his picture, and he is more dependent on how he selects his image from a given chaotic environment. While a photograph can be appreciated for all the traditional methods of organization — use of perspective, balance of shapes, triangles, leading lines — a particularly relevant way to read photographs is to examine the way that framing is used.

What is included or excluded from the picture becomes important and the placement of the centre of interest to what, by implication, is happening outside the frame. The subject can be centrally placed in the picture, be contained and removed from the action of the world outside the frame. Thus set apart its importance is enhanced. This can present a satisfying wholeness. Conversely, the photographer can work increasingly toward the edge of his frame, even using the edge to cut off objects, partially or completely removing clues as to form, scale or position in space, frustrating the viewer's ability to interpret the 'reality' of the picture. Thus, ambiguity and tension is intensified. The eye is moved around the edge of the picture setting up a competing area of interest to the centre; or the activity at the edge can draw the eye out of the picture to imagine an action or form just outside the frame.

A frame can be placed within the picture itself, focusing attention on what is contained within it, as if it were a completely separate picture in its own right. What is within such an internal frame might be very important to the content of the picture, or, if it isn't, the mere fact that it is 'framed' elevates it to an importance that the viewer feels he must justify. Similarly, pictures have been organized like a diptych or triptych, creating relationships between the panels, offering unexpected juxtapositions, demanding a connection be made, telling a story metaphorically.

Atget's *A l'homme armé* is ostensibly a record of a Paris shop front, its grille-work, ornamentation and sign. However, it is also a picture that gains if one looks at its frames. From the sculptural emblem in its niche above the door, one quickly goes to the door itself and the people framed by the window; from the elegant moustache on the helmeted man of the sign to that of the waiter behind the glass. One then looks further into the window to see into the shop, into the picture, in order to decipher what isn't so clear, the almost tranparent second waiter. One also looks into the other frames, the window with its ornaments and the hirsute bosses above. The eye has been led into the picture and takes over, looking at each surface, each detail, to discover more.

Robert Frank's *Trolley, New Orleans (page 30)* is an amazing picture in its uncanny marriage of form and content. On one level it is a slice of everyday America. On another level it graphically presents the social reality of racial segregation in the U.S. South where blacks rode separated from whites at the rear of the bus. (Are the window mullions a visual pun: white bars?). Like the ages of man it also shows the separation of men from each other: man from woman from child from black, each frame displaying a different facial expression. Every area of the surface is made interesting, each panel a separate picture that can be examined individually, from the abstract reflections in each of the upper windows to the muted, contrapuntal rhythms of light and rivets below. Stieglitz' *Steerage,* by being split by the gangway, implies a dichotomy between classes of immigrants on board the boat (being looked down upon from a third space — Stieglitz and camera in first class). But this strong dividing form also sets up relationships between the other forms in the picture, the angle of the funnel and the ladder, the white erose space between the people on the top deck pointing as it were to the straw boater highlighted by the sun on the man looking down and the shapes created by the shawls of the women below.

Bruce Davidson's picture from *East 100th Street (page 81)* contrasts the huddled Puerto Rican couple in the dark interior of the building with the city outside. Friedlander's *Connecticut (page 31)* by its strong slicing into three panels by poles on the street demands that connections be made, in what on the surface is the most banal of street scenes, between the war memorial soldier poised over two middle-aged women, haunting and stalking, and the young women and child in the next frames.

The trio of pictures by Cartier-Bresson, Danny Lyon *(page 32),* and Robert Adams *(page 33)* achieve a coherence through the rhythm of shapes in the picture. The pattern of windows and heads in Cartier-Bresson's *Madrid;* the pattern of roadside bollards with rounded tops, windbloated shapes on the motorcycles and the insulators on the telephone poles in Lyon's *Wisconsin;* and Adam's *Alameda Ave.* is almost literally tied together by the thin spider web of telephone wires and the rhythm of pendant lamps and roadside poles.

34 Robert Frank

40 Lee Friedlander

43 Danny Lyon

44 Robert Adams

Abstraction and Ambiguity of Space

It is difficult to say why abstraction pleases the mind. Partially it is the satisfaction of solving a puzzle, relating the abstract to the reality as we feel we know it. The schematic ordering of actuality meets the desire of the mind to see things whole and not in chaos. In photography, the movement of the camera above or below normal eye-level alters the way the subject appears on the film surface. Lenses flatten spatial relations into patterns on the two dimensional surface, the camera is placed so that key lines run into each other destroying perspective clues and confusing identity of forms, the subject is framed so as to eliminate ready indications as to space and scale. Ambiguity of spatial relations, as with ambiguity in content attracts the mind like a magnet. It arouses curiosity and a desire to learn about the object. A tension is created between the accurate record one expects and the unexpected dimensions and relationships depicted.

Coburn's *The Octopus* is an early example of taking an unusual vantage point which not only shows a view of the scene we would not ordinarily have observed but also a pleasing well-composed abstract pattern. In the *Railroad Station (page 35)* Kertesz uses strong light as well as a high vantage point to stress the pattern of abstract forms. While the man in white along the platform seems to lose all bearing in space, the platform tilts up towards the picture-plane and the man is transformed into a floating shape.

Not only is one fascinated by the fine detail of Atget's *Corsets,* the nostalgic look into the past and the rhythm of the repeated shapes, but there is an added note of mystery. It is almost as if the corseted dummy outside the shop had just flown out from among its sister corsets inside the window, an allusive spatial ambiguity, enhanced by a hint of motion in the blurred cloth beneath it. One wonders, in a photograph of such superb composure, what has moved that cloth, a ghost?

The texture of surfaces, especially that of walls has continually occupied the photographer. Similarly pattern, sets up a rhythm for the eye to follow, stimulates the eye and leads it over the picture surface, linking together otherwise disparate parts of the image. Walker Evans' *Sidewalk and Shopfront (page 38)* not only presents a dominant, almost humorous, relation between the zebra stripes on the woman's blouse and those of the barber shop, but the patterns on the very edges of the picture pick up from the pattern in the centre and lead the eye around the perimeter so that all parts of the picture are imbued with interest; the car and its headlamp, a similar shape in the panel of the door, the Chinese script, the balcony grille-work, the shutters, the railing on the corner of another balcony, even the pattern of the brickwork, and back again to the shop and woman — a theme and variations.

48 André Kertesz

46 Ira W. Martin

49 Kevin Keegan

38

59 Walker Evans

58 Lewis Baltz

Surrealism

Almost all photographs and almost all those in the show are surrealist to the extent that they contain some mystery or problems beyond reality to fascinate the viewer. The surrealist object is full of suggestion, and surrealism in photography is that which presents a wealth of innuendo, setting in motion an emotional response far richer than the straight story confined by logical thought processes. The surrealist image is to be comprehended, not explained. The photographs in this section of the show are not exclusively surrealist but deal with many of the elements that are surrealist: humour, nonsense, fascination, dream, an appeal to the subsconscious and irrationality. It is a world where objects and ideas are not fully fashioned but where images and our idea of them are undergoing constant change, appearing and disappearing, replete with apparent accident. Photographs in this mode shock and surprise to intensify experience, destroy preconceived standards and evoke new impressions and ideas. They are more real than real, transcending the mere recording of reality. Even photography's facility for recording precisely and accurately can produce a clarity that is unreal, or more poetically, surreal.

Humour and juxtaposition are basic tools and can be used to make a social comment or merely stress the strangeness of accident. Friedlander's picture *(page 47)* of a 'laughing dog' becomes increasingly humourous as one notices elsewhere and everywhere in the picture forms echoing the dog's open mouth: the shadow of a street sign on the white corner block, the shadow of the fire hydrant, the angles made by the traffic lights, and the white stripes painted on the roadway. Every angle laughs with the dog and the picture becomes a game of discovery. Even the tree silhouette in the background suggests a rather Snoopy-like dog with his mouth ajar and the Dog House hot-dog stand seems almost a detail too much — a bad pun line.

Shahn's picture of an Ozark sharecropper family *(page 42)* can give the bizarre sensation that the child is more doll-like than the doll and that it is the doll that is the child of poverty. This in no way detracts from the wonderful face of the mother, from the Virgin Mother and Child allusion of the composition, nor from the intricacy of the lines centering around the mother's hands. But one returns to the amazing similarity of the mother's lively face looking off one way and the doll's with a matching intentness looking off in the other direction. It is the doll that shows the same lively twinkle as the mother while the baby is hauntingly lifeless and anomic.

Brandt's *Tic Tac Men (page 44)* elicits an unreal dreamlike mood. So do Winogrand's *Dallas, Texas* and Tony Ray-Jones' *Brook Street. W.1.* The viewer can only stop and ask, ''What's going on here?'' The images suggest disorder, dream, sadism perhaps, or at least a certain amount of evil afoot, touching, like a Kafka novel, on subconscious fears.

Many photographs may be the product of accident or improvisation but still assault our traditional habits of seeing and suggest a welter of associations. The eerie obliteration of the face of the basket vendor in Atget's photograph with a puff of smoke like a question mark instead. Mark Edwards' picture *(page 46)* of a publicity stunt for the film King Kong, a frame that has been light-struck at the end of the roll of film obliterating just the faces of the men, leaving isolated the gestures of the hands now disconnected from facial expressions for which we automatically search to give meaning to the men's actions. Disconnection and a hint of science fiction, as the whimsical idea occurs that the men are really extraterrestrial beings emanating rays that mar the film. A fantasy world to compound that of King Kong and Hollywood.

69 Ben Shahn

67 Clarence John Laughlin

43

44

72 Josef Koudelka

76 Mark Edwards

65 Lee Friedlander

Sequences

"Two statements are made *as if* they were connected, and the reader is forced to consider their relations for himself . . . He will invent a variety of reasons why these facts should have been selected and *order them* in his own mind . . . (the) essential fact about the poetical use of language". William Empson, *Seven Types of Ambiguity.*

In the same way that a frame or division in a picture can imply a relationship that had not existed previously, two or more pictures put together or in sequence can give a more intense view than a single picture, the whole being more than the sum of its parts.

Photography has increasingly moved away in recent years from the simple, or possibly not so simple, series of pictures telling an anecdotal or narrative story, to more complex ways of juxtaposing images, and away from objective reporting to a more personal, internal vision.

Elliott Erwitt's old man encountering a disinterested dog has a nice sense of humour and humanity (and canine-inity) but is well in the genre of the conventional photojournalistic picture essay. Duane Michals *Chance Meeting,* on the other hand, uses the viewer's assumptions about seeing reality in a photograph but is an internal fantasy acted out for the camera. It probably leaves the person looking at the photograph a lot more to speculate about, both in terms of what is happening and what the state of mind of the photographer is, than Erwitt's saga. It is story-telling on a more thought-provoking level.

Doisneau's two pictures of a wedding party, *(page 50),* humourous and ironic — the photographer taking the picture of the photographer taking the picture — also has other levels of meaning. Not only is it about time and the vanished event but like a textbook illustration it bares the structure of the event; again the exposé of reality and, perhaps, a photographer's personal comment on his craft. The second picture fully reveals the structure of the bleachers that the wedding party was posed on and the structure of the tree stripped bare of its leaves; the photographer's black viewing cloth is thrown back to bare the mechanism of the camera. Even in the bareness of the structures the legs of the tripod echo the triangular support of the wooden stand, implying a structural relationship between the seats and the camera that underlay the live, human relationship present in the first photograph between the photographer and the wedding guests.

A number of photographers have subtly organized books of their pictures into a pictorial story line, a novelette of images instead of words. Walker Evans did this in his 1938 book, *American Photographs,* building up a commentary on image making, in effect on photography itself. Robert Frank's *The Americans,* too, is arranged so as to intensify the photographer's penetrating view of the American way of life. Not only does he have "chapter headings" (using pictures containing an American flag) and development of character in the elaboration and repetition of a number of social symbols, such as the juke box, but he also narrates small episodes that enhance his key images. Many have seen in isolation the powerful picture of the covered car in *Long Beach, Cal. (page 52)* and intuitively felt that it was a symbol, in some way, of American culture but have found it difficult to say why. Some have ventured to see the cover, the portable garage, as more than an indication of the luxury Americans can lavish on their cars and seen it as a shroud. The meaning, however, is enhanced if one looks at it as part of a sequence of pictures which one might title 'death on the highway'. This sequence begins with the throw of a dice, a gamble, continues with the act of setting off for a drive in a car and the omnipresence of the automobile (the ironic desire of people to sit and relax amidst the din and fumes of traffic). The meaning of the shrouded car is made painfully clearer by the ensuing picture *(page 53)* of victims of a highway accident on a stretcher covered with a blanket. The dénouement of this episode is the endless road stretching off into the desert which becomes a symbol of America itself, haunted empty space and scalelessness.

Josephson's pictures *(page 51)* if juxtaposed as here, show a relationship between forms which prompt a purely visual association between the paint on the wall and the patterns caused by the windblown bush that is completely independent of verbal narrative. David Watt, too, has taken a couple of found snapshots and mounted them together so that they play on all the viewer's associations about reflections and the sea, frustrating the obvious, inviting creative storytelling.

82 Robert Doisneau

50

84 Kenneth Josephson

85 Kenneth Josephson

51

79 Robert Frank

80 Robert Frank

Light

Light is so essential to photography that it is a wonder that so little can be said about it in words. The eye itself is constantly reacting to light and is always startled to see the infinite changes and permutations that occur in everyday life. Light reveals the unfamiliar and alters the familiar; it can make the ordinary unusual. Its patterns can create order or fragment a whole into new patterns. It evokes associations, moods and emotions.

Light can be the means of imbuing the subject with meaning, atmosphere, poetic qualities; or light can be the subject per se to which the photograph addresses itself. Atget's photograph of a light bulb in the stairwell at *11 Rue du Cherche-Midi,* becomes more than a record of the graceful floral forms of the railing and light bracket; it becomes about light itself, adding a mystical life to the picture. It rivets one's attention and becomes almost psychodelic, floating in the space it has created for itself, at times floating out of the picture towards the viewer. In the same way, Keith Collie's picture of light bulbs *(page 59)* examines the light source itself, more than the quality of light and the way it illumines or dramatizes the subject.

Raking across the surface of a building, light reveals its textures, volumes and forms, intensifying the fineness of its details, as in Abbott's *Cigar Store;* or it can suffuse the picture entirely with an atmosphere, as in Walker Evans' *Post Office at Sprott, Ala.* In this latter picture the light is everywhere, evoking the turgid warmth of a hot summer day in the South and adding a luminescence even to the wall of the building that is in shadow. The light is not specific, but it is omnipresent, and like the opalescence of a pearl adds its own beauty to the photograph which has enough oddities of content, space and time to keep the viewer gripped. (The scale of the petrol pumps, gigantic? The dimensions of the room above the porch — for a midget? And how would one enter that mysterious room and for what purpose was it built?). In Raymond Moore's *Cyprus (page 58),* light defines and articulates. Each form in the picture is picked up and handled by the light and presented to the spectator as a precious object — not laundry, but items worthy of being displayed under glass at the British Museum.

Light can also be graphic, selecting areas of vision or creating patterns that cut across the subject matter of the photograph, superimposing a second vision over the first, as in Josephson's *Chicago (page 57).* The converse of light is shadow, the abstract patterns made by light's absence, revealing new shapes, abstracted shapes, distorted shapes, providing punctuation to the text, enhancing the rhythms of the image; bold and stark as in Strand's *Wall Street,* with man blotted out and abstracted in the street of money, or rich and varied as in Welpott's *San Francisco.*

95 René Burri

92 Bill Brandt

96 Kenneth Josephson

97 Raymond Moore

98 Keith Collie

Naturally, one does not look at a photograph just to see how well it is constructed. One can never lose sight of how the whole comes together, the subject matter itself, the attitude of the photographer to what he is photographing and what the photograph expresses. In looking at the way photographers have interpreted the city, we see a tremendous shift of attitudes toward the subject along a number of lines. If one were to generalize, one could trace a movement away from the romantic view of the city as a remarkable creation of man, to an alienated view of the city, a destroyer of man. Photographers have shifted from portraying their subject matter as grand and heroic to exposing the commonplace and tawdry; from a city of atmosphere to one antiseptic in its clarity; from an ordered environment to a chaotic one, or from a largely rich ambience to a sparse empty one. In this the spirit of man can loom large or can be reduced to nothing, oppressed and made invisible by its surroundings.

Atget's *Court, Rue de Valence (page 64)* serenely composed, with meticulous detail, gives the viewer the feeling of having just chanced by. The slight angle the picture is taken at belies the fact that it was taken with a large-format camera fixed on a tripod. Instead, the angle gives the picture the feeling of having been caught by accident just as though Atget were casually passing. Though the car, the motorcycles and the parts lying around the courtyard are signs of ordinary everyday life, as if the men had just knocked off for lunch, they have such composure that they belong and are integrated with the ancient buildings surrounding them. One feels that the photographer had great affection for the objects he was recording.

Tice's *Hudson Fish Market and Absecon Lighthouse (page 65)* is a latter day effort at recording the ordinariness of the city but it shows a city that is no longer of one wholeness. A plethora of nondescript architecture is tossed together into a salad of forms and the most fascinating element becomes the thin rhythm of the telephone wires, the foot spikes on the pole, the laundry lines, the TV aerials, and the wiry crown on top of the lighthouse. The purer form of the lighthouse has been hidden by the purposeless development of the city; the telephone wires, for better or worse, dominate the scene. From Atget, the involved, almost loving commentator, we have moved towards Tice the seemingly dispassionate and detached viewer. Instead of creating a unitary volume of space, Tice has recorded a fragmented, abstracted space, more of planes than of volumes. The viewer is not invited to enter the picture, nor made comfortable. The apparent serenity of the scene is not one exuding life, rather it seems to be the result of a vacuum.

More coldly removed, with a very sophisticated beauty and wit and a concern with technical sharpness and clarity is Nixon's view of New York, *View Toward Midtown from Wall Street. (page 66).* It is a fascinating picture. Pinpoint clarity is one of the mystifying properties of photography; it makes the image realer than real; it demands that the viewer search to see into the farthest reaches of the print and identify each detail. Within the picture, with what one can only term wit, is an element that reinforces this challenge to the viewer. There is an odd flash of white in the distance which at first glance seems to be some spilled chemical on the negative which has left a blotch on the image. But, on closer examination, one can see that it contains details, those of the lights of a city avenue. Then one sits back and marvels at how that light defies perspective and like a banner whips out of its proper space. However, the view is a very cool, almost emotionless look at the city, very precise, very orderly with a wry fillip that is not about the city at all but rather about the games the photographer wishes to play with his photography. Although Atget's print is equally detailed, it exudes a warmer quality than Nixon's.

Killip's *Playground (page 67),* though also highly detailed, expresses his point in yet a different way. The picture tends to be dominated by the huge electric pylon. In an attempt to find meaning in the image, one searches the contour of the skyline, follows the angle of wires, the fencing and the tops of the concrete fence posts until one is led finally to the angles of the seats on the playhorse behind the fence. This forlorn children's playhorse on a barren concrete base, almost emerges from a fenced-in murk, a children's playground lost in the industrial-urban environment.

105 Paul Outerbridge, Jnr.

108 Walker Evans

112 Eugène Atget

113 George A. Tice

110 Nick Nixon

114 Chris Killip

View of Humanity

"... Contemporary vision, the new life, is based on an honest approach to all problems, be they morals or art. False fronts to buildings, false standards in morals, subterfuge and mummery of all kinds, must be, will be scrapped." *The Daybooks of Edward Weston.*

As with the view of the city, the attitude of the photographer toward humanity within the city seems to move along a scale from romantic to cynical (or clinical) realism, reflecting an increasing feeling of anomie in an urban environment. While the view of the photographer towards the actuality before his camera has shifted, he is also consciously or unconsciously challenging old ways of composing the picture (to *some* it would seem it is a march with all deliberate speed toward randomness, chaos, or just boring nothingness). Nevertheless, it must be examined as part of the attempt to spur the viewer to look longer at the picture, think harder, and have new experiences.

Photographers have tended to move away from letting people be the object of the picture, classically composed and focused on, to using them as means to express his own, inward looking, personal view. There is a tendency for photographers to document themselves, considering their own persona of more importance than the search for individuality in others. The subject is no longer 'hero' to be celebrated, as Strand continued to do throughout his life. In his *Family, Luzzara, Italy* he has taken the ordinary people and made them extra-ordinary. Rather, people in photographs have increasingly become 'anti-hero'; they are us. Such are the faces in the street by William Klein.

Hine's *Danny Mercurio (page 72),* despite the fact that it is a picture of a ragamuffin newspaper boy, with a nice contrast in both form and costume between the raggedness of the boy and the neatness of the matron passing by, despite the implied social comment and look at 'child labour', the paper boy is centrally placed in the picture, faced full on. There is a full confrontation and, in a way, respect for the person photographed. Similarly, Brandt's *East End Girl* is observed for what she is. Informality though has increasingly been sought, to stress, in effect, that this is reality not a pose.

Other currents can be noticed. People in photographs become more randomly placed within the picture as in Tony Ray-Jones' *Ramsgate (page 73),* or increasingly dispersed toward the edges. It is as if the well-composed, centrally oriented subject is suspect, unreal, and that randomness better sugests the uncontrolled events that are now felt to be reality. Ultimately figures get amputated by the frame, or the figures are faceless, shown from the rear, obliterated by shadows or blocked out by the street furniture of the city, as in Friedlander's *Chicago, 1966 (page 75).* The fragmentation of the picture's organization reflects the photographer's reaction and attitude to the society around him. This is not to say that photography has followed a linear development toward these ends but that photographers have continued to explore new ways—both formally and in attitude—to express man's relationship to the society in which he lives. The photographs criticize the commonplace, yet at the same time can elevate it to something that can be valued, an ambiguous situation.

Brassai's *Bijou of Montmartre (page 70)* not only tells us about this woman by directly looking at her face but also by examining the details of her clothing, her jewellery, her make-up, the way she holds her hand. While we may reasonably conclude that she is a demi-mondaine, there is a tremendous feeling of respect in the photo for the individual; whereas, a portrait in a similar mode by Lisette Model conveys a certain oddity about the woman with the veil, an attitude that she is a freak, someone pitiable. One wonders if there isn't a bit of the snide superiority of the voyeur in the person taking the picture rather than sympathy toward the subject. Friedlander's self-portrait *(page 71),* his shadow on the back of the girl he is following, is hardly a concern about the subject but solely about the photographer's attempt to seek identity with this anonymous person, an existentialist object that stresses by the harsh light its separateness from the photographer.

129 Brassaï

127 Lee Friedlander

116 Lewis Hine

120 Tony Ray-Jones

123 Manuel Alvarez Bravo

124 Lee Friedlander

Photographs - Demands and Expectations. Peter Turner

Looking at photographs is my occupation, my preoccupation and my pleasure. To see a good photograph is a joy, to view a great one can transport me to another quite separate dimension. Gazing at some seemingly innocent transcript of the world particular to the photographer at that moment when the image was made, I can become as another person. I am held suspended somewhere between reality and illusion, excited while what is public and visible — the content of this picture — is mysteriously and compellingly intertwined with a private and previously hidden understanding of how the world appears to another. And this other person I become, exists and extends its being beyond the confines of the print, as I assume a fresh identity, an alter ego, myself and yet in part the maker of the photograph, as image and imagining join together in a place between space and time.

Great photographs have taken me further and deeper than I could go alone. They are music and poetry, they are of a language richer and more profound than simple words. At their height they can tap a rare source and speak about the very essence of life. As the foundation of the fine arts has been the bringing together, resolving and making equal of the opposites of existence, so photography can use fact as a metaphor to create new fact, draw the tacit from the explicit and use the outer to reveal the inner. At its most potent, this medium, with all the connotations of absolute verity that we have come to associate with it, can be the means by which we are able to see the unseen. Its true delights are beyond verbal description, they have eluded even the most eloquent, but as a constant looker at photographs, let me attempt at least to deal with some of the clues and code-words that make up its language and the syntax of camera vision.

A photograph is an equation of light, space and time. It can use these elements in an almost abstract sense so becoming a celebration of a particular quality. In Raymond Moore's picture, for example, *Cyprus (page 58)* light — the generative force of the medium — becomes the substance of the image. A subtle, yet revealing and luminescent light that defines and articulates the surface of a building, suggestive in its action of possibilities beyond the façade, while giving dimension to the content as a whole. Equally and perhaps more commonly, the elements are used together, interwoven as the various facets of the picture are choreographed and seen in harmony. Here light becomes the vehicle; supportive of the photographer's concept, space the context and time the incisor, creating the discrete moment in which the nature of the image can be seen. But these are primary considerations of a very basic nature — a photograph is born of these and more, for it is the sometimes unwilling marriage of man and machine and the way of seeing particular to the camera that has allowed us to experience a vision separate from standard human perception.

At its strongest, photography is the art of the real. Since its beginnings the sheer fascination of the photograph has been with its nearness to reality, its perfection in delineation, its suggestion of absolute truthfulness. And yet the camera can subvert reality by its absolute impartiality. Even with the most meticulous attention to composition and the subtlest use of graphic devices, its lack of selectivity (other than framing and focus by the photographer) will render the insignificant as importantly as the significant. Unlike a human the camera ignores nothing and what we see as viewers of a photograph is not what we could have perceived as observers at the original scene. Thus for the photographer the opportunities exist for learning what his camera will see and recognising the conflict between this and the real world. He can explore the tensions of the separate reality that dislocates his image from common perceptual experience. By virtue of his ability to abstract some personally vital moment from the continuum and instill into it a sense of order and direction, he can, in effect, allow the viewer to share in a world composed of the familiar, yet referring to something unique. In this lies something of my excitement for looking at photographs. I must confront a paradox, as I see the commonplace and everyday charged with a special kind of poetry, as reality and illusion join forces.

This may seem a small, almost insignificant point. And yet I believe it to be of singular importance. We are surrounded by photographs, we have been since we were born. We know what a photograph is, we recognise its physical make-up. We have almost certainly taken a photograph, just as we have equally probably been part of one. In short, we believe we know what to expect. And because our demands are linked to our expectations, we will possibly demand too little or simply retire with a sense of confusion if a photograph does not fit neatly into those preconceptions. To be sure, photographs can and sometimes do shake our accepted manner of viewing the world in a very direct way. Russell Sorgi's picture of a suicide *(page 18)* is a dramatic example Caught between life and death, a girl's body is halted in a curiously unemotional fashion. With the full expectation of the horror we know to be following removed, we can consider the allusions made by the picture in a calm and unhurried state, free from all responsibility of actual presence at the scene. But few photographs deal with such an enactment of crisis. In the main, they are of a less overtly forceful nature that does not, at first glance, seem to warrant the detailed examination that is essential to gain from them as much as possible. Hence the sense of confusion that I mentioned — photographs can work simultaneously on several levels and if we view them only for what they appear to offer on the surface, we will lose their greater potential.

So, if we temporarily abandon our existing understanding of what are the concerns of a photographic image and accept that it may involve more than appears on the surface, how then are we to approach it? One answer, as I mention above, may come from a recognition of how our comparative sophistication has deluded us and led us to think that we 'know' what constitutes a photograph. If we look back at public reaction to the invention of photography, we find an immediate response to this new way of picturing the world that can offer some suggestions. In the *New York Monthly Magazine* of December 1839, shortly after the announcement of Daguerre's discovery of a photographic process, the editor Lewis Gaylord Clark enthuses on daguerreotypes he had seen in Paris. "Mark the minute light and shade; the perfect clearness of every object . . . The shade of a shadow is frequently reflected in the river . . . The very trees are taken with the shimmer created by the breeze — a segment of time has been allowed to trace its movement across the surface of the photograph, enough for us to bear witness to the energy and the flux of life." With an understanding uninterrupted by the conventions of photographic tradition, Clark allowed himself to be entranced by the subtle frankness those images showed, astonished by how, with some strange chemical magic, he was able to witness an almost surreal transformation and transfixation of the world external to the camera. In his hands he could hold a tiny replica of life, open to inspection, ready for dissection. And immediately he began to consider how that reproduction reality of minute detail went beyond what could be seen in front of the camera and began to create a new kind of reality, an actuality free from the vagaries of human perception.

Clark's recognition of the significance of fact within a photograph is an excellent point to begin the journey towards its meaning. But, as I mentioned before, photographs can work on several levels and to reach the core we must ask more of an image than an enquiry as to the way it looks will reveal. What to photograph, how and why are the immediate questions that the image-maker must ask, and these in turn form the basis for the viewer's consideration of a picture. For the non-photographer the method of making a photograph is only slightly relevant and, in any case, outside the scope of this essay. What actually constitutes the picture is also outside my brief, as it is covered elsewhere. Suffice to say that the central problem is one of selection, the act of choice on the part of the photographer and how what is included in a picture will allude to what is excluded and vice versa. Beyond this, we are left with the illusive 'why'? If a photograph is about something more than a visual record of the way things appear to the unblinking impartiality of the camera, what is its purpose?

By now it must be obvious that I am concerned to stress the limiting nature of a concept of the photograph as a form of surrogate reality. While they do function as a valuable informational source, many photographers are concerned to express more than simple fact in their images. To paraphrase Edward Weston, it must be the thing itself and yet more than just 'the thing'. Perhaps the first point of departure is for them to become involved in picturing some form of emotional response, or maybe to record some aesthetic pleasure. As their vision matures so their photographs begin to contain a commentary — light is no longer simply 'light' but begins to hold a specific delight; the city is no longer just a 'city' but becomes a symbol, a monument to man and so on. As the complexities of the image increase, so does its potential for communicating some profundity, until it can be viewed as a multi-layered statement speaking of the photographer's intention, understanding and realisation in some concrete form. But there is still the possibility for a photograph to transcend even these elaborate stages in its construction, for we are thinking of it in cold mechanical terms that are almost contradictory of a product of human sensibilities. As I mentioned at the beginning of this piece, at its highest a picture can deal with some aspects of the very nature of life itself.

Looking at a photograph, we see first its outer covering, a shell that can offer an immediate aesthetic gratification, then, searching further, we can find detail, the particulars of which mark not only its deeper significance but also its absolute involvement with the photographic medium. And if we venture further, we begin to encounter the true richness that the photograph can offer. Hidden deep within it lies an image of the person who made it, that promises contact on a level that I find impossible in any other form of expression. This is my true excitement with photography — the photograph is not simply a window on the world through which we may stare with a vision borrowed from its maker, it is more a mirror that reflects back the demands we make of it together with this image of the photographer. In viewing Robert Frank's work, for example, I can slip behind the social insight, visual dexterity and structural dynamism and share in the experience of being Robert Frank. The same is true with Lee Friedlander, whose camera-constructed vision of the urban scene has done so much to enlarge the visual vocabulary of the medium — within his images exist clues to the nature of being Lee Friedlander. The same is true, in fact, of all those pictures that I regard as being 'good' or 'great' by photographers known and unknown. Those photographers enter into a relationship with photography outside of any commitment to subject matter that demands a total honesty of approach. Through their pictures they must ' lay themselves on the line', expose themselves, make themselves vunerable. Only in this way can they hope to make pictures of integrity and lasting worth.

Looking at photographs can be as simple or as complex as we and the pictures care to make it. But, as with so many areas of life, I think it would be true to say that the more you give, the more you get. And so far I remain undisappointed.

39 Bruce Davidson

Photographic Time and "The Real World." Ian Jeffrey

Commentators and critics usually agree that photographs make particular claims on our attention but they are rarely specific as to the nature of these claims. Even as they agree, most continue to regard photography as little more than a kind of painting, sufficiently similar to be considered in much the same terms. After all, many photographs look like paintings and are even intended to do so. Furthermore, the two affect us in very similar if not exactly identical ways. There are enough affinities to allow us, without too much trouble, to consider photographs as though they were paintings. No one would think this sort of consideration to be entirely absurd; indeed in some cases, especially with the grander Victorian photographs, it is even necessary if the point of the image is to be taken. On the other hand, it would be patently absurd to consider paintings as though they were photographs. Which is to say, that although there are affinities, there is also a radical difference and unless this difference is recognised, many photographs will continue to be taken in other than their own terms.

What is this difference? At first sight it may seem to involve nothing more than the photograph's greater accuracy. Yet a naturalistic painting can be as informative and exact as any photograph and a painted portrait can give extraordinary access to character. Even so, by comparison with photographs such portraits remain inauthentic, no matter how scrupulous and revealing they may be. In some way then, the photograph is existentially true and convincing, as other images are not. Somehow the photograph not only presents things as though they are there but mysteriously it presents the things themselves. Thomas Hardy refers to this profound ambiguity in a poem of around 1913 called *The Photograph.* He recounts his feelings on burning an old photograph ''in a casual clearance of life's arrears.'' To his astonishment he finds himself crying out with hurt and averting his eyes as the flame eats its way through the portrait. Something of the life of the subject is preserved in the image, absorbed or taken at the moment of the image's making.

Hardy is acknowledging in his way, what we acknowledge in passing, when we refer to the ''taking'' of a photograph. Although by now this verb is used automatically and vaguely in this context, it still carries with it ideas of removal and seizure, even if the only people who recognise this clearly are those legendary tribesmen who, either out of superstition or self-respect, still object to the taking of their pictures.

What it is precisely which is taken is open to question. It is an image but one in which the subject remains interfused and this is the principal sense in which photographs differ from paintings. It follows that, in certain respects, a photograph, or what appears in it, exists for us as the original subject once existed. This makes it natural, in front of a photograph, to wonder both about the moment at which the image was taken and the setting from which it was taken. One might speculate but only fancifully, in front of a Rubens or a Rembrandt on what happened before and after the event but in front of Russell Sorgi's *Suicide (page 18)* this sort of speculation is a crucial part of our apprehension of the picture. Such an image raises insistent questions about motive and aftermath. So too does Rembrandt in his horrifying painting of *The Blinding of Samson* but less insistently; the painting is evidently a construct, a fabrication, and this qualifies the horror of the moment. It is a matter of paint and artifice, as well as a record of an event.

This explains why we are usually prepared to accept the moments represented in paintings without further explanation whereas we expect photographs of this sort to be accompanied by an explanation of the circumstances in which the image was taken. In this way the image is completed; or at least, it is situated within the wider time and place of the event and so ceases to be a mere fragment. The text, either the writer's story or the photographer's explanation, invokes experience of normal time which is denied by the photographic instant. The image is, as it were, domesticated; it becomes less disconcerting, less of an affront to our expectations. On the other hand, to present such an image without benefit of text is to draw attention to the unfamilar nature of photographic time. This means that the nature of the medium itself can be disclosed. Thus, in addition to providing a report on an event, the image can be used reflexively, as a way of pointing to the medium through which the report is made. Something of this sort is demonstrated by Cartier-Bresson in his picture of 1932, *Behind St. Lazare (page 15)* where he catches the moment between leap and impact. With surrounding time referred to but not recorded, the moment is isolated and the incident uncompleted. The photograph is an intervention in time and time disrupted in this way is time made strange and thereby brought to our attention.

Such images work because they are disquieting, even bizarre. Time is brought to a standstill at the most unlikely moments and the photograph stands out unmistakably as a fragment snatched from the continuum. It is not that the continuum is denied but rather implied or entailed, just as any fragment entails the complete figure to which it belongs. Many photographers, however, have been unwilling to rely on this kind of implication, preferring rather to enclose time within the image.

In everyday experience, time appears to be articulated by the transition from darkness into light and back again. This has its spatial equivalent in the monochrome of the photograph. Time can thus be transformed and gathered into the black and white of the image. This is true of any monochrome photograph, although it is not always evident except in those images where the extremes of black and white are set out and connected by a plenitude of half-tones. Such photographs can be said to embody those transitions between darkness and light which are the transitions of the day and of time in general. Edward Weston is the great example of a photographer intent on the space-time transformation attainable in monochrome images.

Completeness of this sort is not gained without sacrifice. Such photographs are equivalents or metaphors; they refer to something which is beyond their compass and in doing so come to refer only partially to the material or scene from which the image is constituted. Enclosing time in general, they cease to refer directly to the instant from which they are taken, or do so only incidentally. The experience which they invoke is of things in general rather than of things in particular, although it is true that they achieve the one by way of the other. Nevertheless Weston and his followers clearly succeed in their quest for the complete and the intact, even if they do place a disproportionate emphasis on the tonal continuum. It could be said that they have gone beyond and by way of photography to abstraction, finding a universal order in the properties of the photograph itself.

By contrast, Walker Evans shows the intact in conjunction with the particular. He was just as interested in and responsive to the tonal continuum as Edward Weston. Evans' photograph of Richard Perkins' corrugated tin facade *(page 26)* is as full of nuanced half-tones as anything printed by Weston but in addition the picture is rich in indices of moment and place. Cast shadows mark the fall of the light, the road marks the extension of the place and the setting of the façade as a frame within the frame marks both Evans' choice of viewpoint and composition. Thus he demonstrates the inter-dependence of photographer, moment and place. The image is made in response to the conjunction of the three; it shows a view of the world and something of how that view arises, whereas Weston shows the vision largely without its ground and its moment. Although both find and acknowledge order and harmony, the difference is that Evans finds this to be manifest in the world and demonstrable through photography, whilst Weston finds and understands exactly the reverse.

Cartier-Bresson, too, has been preoccupied with the problem of order and the instant. Indeed it may have been a more insistent problem for him than for either Evans or Weston. Whilst they have singled out things and scenes which are to a certain extent pre-arranged and complete in themselves and which they then seek to acknowledge in photography, he by contrast has focused on flux and movement, yet still found that an order displays itself. Out of a mass of snapshots certain images emerge as more successful than others. They are successful because they are more complete, a blend of figure and setting. To account for this he has evolved the theory of "the decisive moment" in which he invokes the idea of a universal harmony. He refers to photography, in the introduction to *Images à la Sauvette* (1952), as implying "the recognition of a rhythm in the world of real things" and to the instinctive fixing of "a geometric pattern without which the photograph would have been both formless and lifeless." And "inside movement," he writes, "there is one moment at which the elements in motion are in balance." This is the moment of equilibrium, the decisive moment.

His theory then, is a metaphysical theory; it has to do with the intuitive identification of an innate order in the world. When this order is embodied, the moment of the photograph is transcended and hence photography is shown to have an important task, to be an art in the full sense of the word. There are distinct affinities between his theory and that of Kandinsky, for example, in which ideas of "inner resonance" are expounded. Although it is not surprising that such a theory should be invoked by an artist, it is surprising that it was invoked, and in these especially metaphysical terms, by a photographer who was also a photo-journalist. One might instead have expected a theory with a narrative bias, in which "the decisive moment" was that instant when individuals or groups gave up their secrets to the detective behind the camera.

Cartier-Bresson probably had such a theory in mind when he came to formulate his idea of "the decisive moment" but as something to be refuted rather than endorsed. Photography had been widely understood since the '30s, as having a revelatory function; human motivation could be studied by means of candid and instantaneous pictures and hence society could be better understood. This is the view of Walter Benjamin outlined in 1931 in his celebrated essay *A Short History of Photography.* He refers to photography as disclosing "the optical unconscious, just as psychoanalysis discloses the instinctual unconscious." Thus we become aware on seeing photographs, of the elements from which vision is constituted and in ways which are forever concealed in normal synthesizing vision. We may, for example, know or be able to characterize the way someone walks, without being able to say anything about the moment when the person starts to walk. That moment can be revealed in photography.

Benjamin was interested in learning secrets; photographs had information to impart. They could yield up the inner truth of personality and what he called: "provenance." He recommended August Sander's work on the grounds that it led to "the training and sharpening of a physiognomic awareness." Anyone schooled in such images would be the better prepared to read the signs of the times and the more equipped for survival, when survival depended on a knowledge of the signs of class and affiliation. This was a tactical recommendation, Benjamin regretted that the times should put such a premium on knowledge of these signs.

He valued Atget on similar tactical grounds. By showing the unconsidered places in the city, Atget stressed the sameness of things in the world and helped destroy our romantic attachment to the spirit of place. And by showing the city empty of its people he brought out those minutiae of place which could be so revealing, yet which were generally overlooked. Thus through photography perception could be sharpened; it had value as a visual aid in an educational context. Cartier-Bresson retained this scheme in outline, although he altered the terms; not only did photographs give access to personal and social secrets but they also disclosed an underlying order in appearance. Thus photographers acknowledged what had always been acknowledged in art.

Whether there is or ever can be a decisive moment is open to question. But what is clear is that photographs constantly refer to far more than they show. They may enclose a greater order in Cartier-Bresson's rhythmic geometry or in Weston's scrupulously realised tonal continuum but even as arbitrary fragments taken from time and place they evoke the greater whole from which they are abstracted.

Bibliographic note. Thomas Hardy's poem   *The Photograph* appears in *Poems of Thomas Hardy: A New Selection,* selected by T.R.M. Creighton, pp.128-129 , London, 1974/ Henri Cartier-Bresson's introduction to *Images à la Sauvette* is reprinted in translation in *Photographers on Photography,* edited by Nathan Lyons, pp.41-51, Englewood Cliffs, New Jersey, 1966/ A translation of Walter Benjamin's *A Short History of Photography* appeared in *Screen* magazine, Spring 1972, volume 13, no. 1, pp.5-26.

Catalogue List
*Photographs illustrated

Time

1. Alfred Stieglitz
The Terminal, 1893
Photogravure on tissue
121 × 158 mm
Loaned by Russ Anderson

*2. Henri Cartier-Bresson
Behind St. Lazare, Paris, 1932
358 × 244 mm
Courtesy Henri Cartier-Bresson/John Hillelson Agency

*3. I. Russell Sorgi
Suicide, 1942
340 × 266 mm

4. André Kertész
Landing Pigeon, N.Y., 1966
349 × 275 mm

*5. Paul Trevor
Fournier St./ Sunday Around Bricklane, 1974
241 × 358 mm

6. Charles Harbutt
Liverpool, 1971
303 × 203 mm

*7. Otto Steinert
Pedestrian, Paris, 1950
290 × 402 mm

*8. William Klein
The Dance, Brooklyn, N.Y., ca. 1955
294 × 400 mm

*9. Eugène Atget
Fair J, n.d.
Reprint by Berenice Abbott from original negative
211 × 161 mm
Loaned by Marlborough Graphics

10. Homer Sykes
London, 1975
169 × 254 mm

Symbol

11. Alfred Stieglitz
The Hand of Man, 1902
Photogravure on plate paper
158 × 214 mm
Loaned by Russ Anderson

12. Ben Shahn
On Duty During Strike, Morgantown, W. Va., 1935
Library of Congress reprint from original negative
262 × 205 mm

*13. Robert Frank
Bar, N.Y., 1955-56
Delpire reprint from copy negative
258 × 388 mm
Loaned by Kunsthaus, Zürich

*14. Garry Winogrand
San Marcos, Texas, 1964
220 × 328 mm

15. Bernard Deschamps
Paris, 1974
122 × 180 mm

16. Paul Strand
Automobile Wheel, N.Y., 1917
Illustration from *Paul Strand: A Retrospective Monograph,* vol. 1
260 × 208 mm

17. Walker Evans
Joe's Auto Graveyard, Pa., 1936
Library of Congress reprint from original negative
102 × 230 mm

18. Henri Cartier-Bresson
Stadium, Milwaukee, Wisc., 1958
241 × 358 mm
Courtesy Henri Cartier-Bresson / John Hillelson Agency

*19. Clarence John Laughlin
The Radiator as a Hand, the Headlight as a Gaping Fish, 1960
272 × 350 mm

20. Art Sinsabaugh
Chicago Landscape No. 117, 1964
132 × 492 mm

21. Lee Friedlander
San Diego, 1970
187 × 281 mm
Loaned by Paul Joyce

22. Brassai
Graffitti, La Masque, 1948
324 × 220 mm

23. Ralph Steiner
Billboard, ca. 1920
Palladium reprint by George A. Tice from the original negative
73 × 100 mm

24. Walker Evans
Torn Movie Poster, 1930
330 × 243 mm
Loaned by Graphics International Ltd.

25. Walker Evans
Houses and Billboards, Atlanta, Ga., 1936
185 × 235 mm

26. Margaret Bourke-White
Kentucky, 1937
243 × 341 mm
Courtesy Life Magazine

27. Nathan Lyons
Untitled, ca. 1963-74
116 × 173 mm

28. Homer Sykes
Gila Bend, 1973
168 × 252 mm

*29. Walker Evans
Corrugated Tin Façade, Moundville, Ala., 1936
191 × 242 mm
Courtesy Walker Evans Estate

*30. Lewis Baltz
West Wall, Unoccupied Industrial Structure, No. 45 the New Industrial
Parks near Irvine, Cal., ca. 1974
153 × 228 mm
Loaned by Graphics International Ltd.

31. Kevin Keegan
Oldham, 1972
268 × 182 mm
Loaned by the Arts Council of Great Britain

Organization of the Picture

32. Eugène Atget
Sign of a Shop: "A l'homme armé," ca. 1903
216 × 169 mm
Loaned by the Victoria and Albert Museum

33. Henri Cartier-Bresson
Seville, 1933
242 × 358 mm
Loaned by Olympus Optical Co.

*34. Robert Frank
Trolley, New Orleans, 1955
Delpire reprint from copy negative
390 × 590 mm
Loaned by Kunsthaus, Zürich

35. Marc Riboud
Peking, 1965
201 × 300 mm

36. David Watt
Untitled, 1975
160 × 109 mm

37. Alfred Stieglitz
The Steerage, 1907
Photogravure
318 × 256 mm
Loaned by Graphics International Ltd.

38. André Kertész
Meudon, 1928
348 × 245 mm

*39. Bruce Davidson
Untitled, East 100th Street, ca. 1970
190 × 253 mm

*40. Lee Friedlander
Connecticut, 1973
188 × 283 mm

41. Lewis Ambler
London, 1976
109 × 162 mm

42. Henri Cartier-Bresson
Madrid, 1933
241 × 357 mm
Courtesy Henri Cartier-Bresson / John Hillelson Agency

*43. Danny Lyon
Route 12 , Wisconsin, 1962
222 × 340 mm

*44. Robert Adams
Alameda Ave., Denver, ca. 1974
149 × 152 mm

Abstraction and Ambiguity of Space

45. Alvin Langdon Coburn
The Octopus, 1912
Reprint from a copy negative, International Museum of Photography,
Rochester, N.Y.
232 × 179 mm

*46. Ira W. Martin (attributed to)
New York, ca. late 1920's
107 × 140 mm
Private collection

47. Ralph Steiner
New York, ca. 1920
Palladium reprint by George A. Tice
91 × 117 mm

*48. André Kertész
Railroad Station, 1937
348 × 274 mm

*49. Kevin Keegan
Oldham, 1972
268 × 182 mm
Loaned by the Arts Council of Great Britain

50. Eugène Atget
Corset Shop, n.d.
Reprint by Berenice Abbott from original negative
Loaned by Marlborough Graphics

51. André Kertész
"Buy," 1962
348 × 252 mm

52. Gerry Badger
Photographer's Shop, Lavender Hill, London, 1974
175 × 135 mm

53. Kenneth Josephson
Chartres, 1972
201 × 305 mm

54. Ralph Steiner
New York, ca. 1920
Palladium reprint by George A. Tice
118 × 92 mm

55. Walker Evans
Scarborough, N.Y., 1931
200 × 156 mm
Private collection

56. Aaron Siskind
Acolman 2, 1955
252 × 320 mm

57. Raymond Moore
Wall Light, 1968
207 × 204 mm
Loaned by Russ Anderson

*58. Lewis Baltz
Xerox Warehousing, No. 27 The New Industrial Parks near Irvine,
Cal., 1974
274 × 192 mm
Loaned by Castelli Graphics

*59. Walker Evans
Sidewalk and Shopfront, New Orleans, 1935
244 × 192 mm
Courtesy Walker Evans Estate

60. Kurt Benning
Untitled, 1975
162 × 240 mm
Loaned by Ian Jeffrey

61. Brassai
Le Dormeur au Canotier sur un Banc, Paris, 1932
204 × 267 mm

62. Paddy Summerfield
Oxford, 1969
164 × 112 mm
Loaned by Peter Turner

Surrealism

63. Eugène Atget
Fête du Trône, n.d.
Reprint by Berenice Abbott from original negative
175 × 225 mm
Private collection

64. Bill Zulpo-Dane
New Orleans, La., 1974
455 × 303 mm

*65. Lee Friedlander
Albuquerque, N.M., 1972
188 × 284 mm

*66. Manuel Alvarez Bravo
Optic Parable, 1931
237 × 180 mm
Loaned by the Victoria and Albert Museum

*67. Clarence John Laughlin
The Portent in the Shadow, 1954
343 × 256 mm

*68. Bill Brandt
Tic Tac Men, Ascot, 1932
335 × 290 mm
Loaned by Marlborough Graphics

*69. Ben Shahn
Wife and Child of Sharecropper, Ozark Mountains, Ark., 1935
Reprint by the Library of Congress from the original negative
165 × 243 mm

70. Garry Winogrand
Dallas, Texas, 1964
221 × 331 mm

71. Tony Ray-Jones
Brook Street, W.1, 1968
140 × 211 mm

*72. Josef Koudelka
Spain, 1971
241 × 359 mm

73. Conrad Hafenrichter
Margate, Kent, 1975
203 × 301 mm

74. Eugène Atget
Street Vendor D, n.d.
Reprint by Berenice Abbott from the original negative
223 × 165 mm
Loaned by Marlborough Graphics

75. Kenneth Josephson
Stockholm, 1967
202 × 305 mm

*76. Mark Edwards
King Kong / "Film Ends," 1976
165 × 245 mm

Sequences

77. Elliott Erwitt
Paris, 1952
Four prints: 304 × 204 mm, 304 × 204 mm, 204 × 305 mm, 204 × 306 mm

78. Robert Frank
U.S. 91 Leaving Blackfoot, Idaho, 1955-6
Delpire reprint from copy negative
258 × 388 mm
Loaned by Kunsthaus, Zürich

*79. Robert Frank
Long Beach, Cal., 1955-6
Delpire reprint from copy negative
262 × 389 mm
Loaned by Kunsthaus, Zürich

*80. Robert Frank
Car Accident, U.S. 66 between Winslow and Flagstaff, Ariz., 1955-6
Delpire reprint from copy negative
254 × 388 mm
Loaned by Kunsthaus, Zürich

81. Robert Frank
Six pages from *Les Americains,* Robert Delpire, Paris, 1958
Elko, Nevada 174 × 115 mm
U.S. 91, Idaho 133 × 201 mm
St. Petersburg, Florida 133 × 201 mm
Long Beach, California 133 × 201 mm
U.S. 66, Arizona 133 × 199 mm
U.S. 285, New Mexico 175 × 115 mm
Loaned by Chris Steele-Perkins

*82. Robert Doisneau
Un Mariage dans le Poitou: Le Photographe, 1957-8
Two prints: 261 × 304, 261 × 304 mm

83. Duane Michals
Chance Meeting, 1969
Six prints: each 85 × 127 mm

*84. Kenneth Josephson
Istanbul, 1972
200 × 307 mm

*85. Kenneth Josephson
San Francisco, 1973
202 × 305 mm

86. David Watt
Assembled Snapshots, 1976
165 × 128 mm

Light

87. Eugène Atget
Hotel de Sully Charost, 11 rue du Cherche-Midi, n.d.
Printing-out paper with gold toning
217 × 173 mm
Private collection

88. Lewis Hine
Mill Running at Night, Whitnel, N.C., 1908
Torn print
120 × 167 mm
Loaned by Graphics International Ltd.

89. Paul Strand
Wall Street, 1915
Photogravure on tissue
132 × 162 mm
Loaned by Russ Anderson

90. Berenice Abbott
Cigar Store, Union Square, N.Y., ca. 1930
190 × 239 mm
Private collection

91. Walker Evans
Post Office, Sprott, Ala., 1936
Reprint by Library of Congress from the original negative
264 × 340 mm

*92. Bill Brandt
London Policeman, 1938
333 × 291 mm
Loaned by Marlborough Graphics

93. Josef Sudek
Janáček House, 1948
162 × 122 mm
Loaned by Sue Davies

94. William Klein
New York, ca. 1955
259 × 387 mm

*95. René Burri
Sao Paolo, 1960
202 × 300 mm

*96. Kenneth Josephson
Chicago, 1961
153 × 227 mm
Loaned by Russ Anderson

*97. Raymond Moore
Cyprus, 1968
163 × 246 mm
Loaned by Bob Hershkowitz

*98. Keith Collie
Untitled, 1972
250 × 197 mm
Loaned by Russ Anderson

99. George A. Tice
Telephone Booth, 3 a.m., Rahway, N.J., 1974
242 × 192 mm

100. Lewis Baltz
R-OHM Corp., No. 26. The New Industrial Parks near Irvine,
Cal., ca. 1974
151 × 258 mm
Loaned by Castelli Graphics

101. Jack Welpott
San Francisco, 1974
174 × 253 mm

102. Guy Ryecart
Hove Seafront, 1976
199 × 137 mm

View of the City

103. Alfred Stieglitz
Flat Iron Building, 1903
Reprint from copy negative, Royal Photographic Society Collection
292 × 145 mm

104. Eugène Atget
Rue Etamine, Beauvais, ca. 1904
210 × 169 mm
Loaned by the Victoria and Albert Museum

*105. Paul Outerbridge, Jnr.
Untitled, 1923
Platinum print
107 × 87 mm
Loaned by Graphics International Ltd.

106. Berenice Abbott
Fifth Avenue at 8th Street, N.Y., n.d.
191 × 241 mm
Loaned by the Marlborough Gallery, New York

107. Bruce Davidson
Untitled, East 100th Street, ca. 1970
253 × 197 mm

*108. Walker Evans
View of Ossining, N.Y., 1930
105 × 198 mm
Private collection

109. Bill Brandt
Rainswept Roofs, 1930's
343 × 283 mm
Loaned by Marlborough Graphics

*110. Nick Nixon
View Toward Midtown from Wall Street, N.Y., 1975
197 × 247 mm

111. Ian Berry
Whitby, Yorkshire, 1975
197 × 295 mm

*112. Eugène Atget
Court, Rue de Valence, 1922
Reprint by Berenice Abbott from original negative
173 × 232 mm
Loaned by Russ Anderson

*113. George A. Tice
Hudson Fishmarket and Absecon Lighthouse, Atlantic City, N.J., 1973
192 × 242 mm

*114. Chris Killip
Playground, 1977
202 × 256 mm

115. Chris Steele-Perkins
New York, 1975
183 × 276 mm

View of Humanity

*116. Lewis Hine
Danny Mercurio, Washington, D.C., 1912
Reprint from a copy negative, International Museum of Photography
Rochester N.Y.
167 × 231 mm

117. Bill Brandt
East End Girl Dancing the Lambeth Walk, 1930's
339 × 291 mm
Loaned by Marlborough Graphics

118. Paul Strand
Family, Luzzara, Italy, 1953
Illustration from *Paul Strand, A Retrospective Monograph,* vol. 2
155 × 198 mm

119. Danny Lyon
Uptown Chicago, 1965
258 × 256 mm

120. Tony Ray-Jones
Ramsgate, 1968
140 × 211 mm.
Loaned by Peter Turner

121. William Klein
Fifth Avenue, Rockefeller Center, N.Y., ca. 1955
282 × 394 mm

122. Harry Callahan
New York, 1969
136 × 215 mm

*123. Manuel Alvarez Bravo
Los Agachados (The Crouched Ones), 1934
184 × 242 mm
Loaned by the Victoria and Albert Museum

*124. Lee Friedlander
Chicago, 1966
169 × 257 mm

125. Colin Curwood
Rykneld Road, Derby, 1972
257 × 198 mm

126. Paul Trevor
London Bridge / City of London - EXIT, 1974
241 × 357 mm

127. Lee Friedlander
New York, 1966
159 × 241 mm
Loaned by Paul Hill

128. Ralph Gibson
Untitled, 1973
317 × 206 mm
Loaned by Ralph Gibson

129. Brassai
"Bijou" of Montmartre, 1932
234 × 258 mm
Loaned by the Victoria and Albert Museum

130. Lisette Model
Woman with Veil, San Francisco, n.d.
492 × 382 mm
Loaned by Graphics International Ltd.

All prints are silver prints unless otherwise noted.
Some undated photographs are listed as being circa the date of their
first publication.

Photography Books from Pantheon

John Berger
About Looking
0-394-73907-8 (paperback)
Another Way of Telling (with Jean Mohr)
0-394-73998-1 (paperback)

Brassaï
The Secret Paris of the Thirties
0-394-73384-3 (paperback)

Richard Cobb
The Streets of Paris
0-394-73865-9 (paperback)

Van Deren Coke
Avant-Garde Photography in Germany
0-394-71052-5 (paperback)

Attilio Colombo
Fantastic Photographs
0-394-73785-7 (paperback)

Andreas Haus
Moholy Nagy: Photographs and Photograms
0-394-50449-6 (hardcover)

Japan Photographer's Association
A Century of Japanese Photography
0-394-51232-4 (hardcover)

Christopher Lyman
The Vanishing Race and Other Illusions:
Photographs of Indians by Edward S. Curtis
0-394-71029-0 (hardcover)

Michael Lesy
Bearing Witness:
A Photographic Chronicle of American Life, 1860-1945
0-394-74942-1 (paperback)
Real Life: Louisville in the Twenties
0-394-73235-9 (paperback)
Time Frames: The Meaning of Family Pictures
0-394-73958-2 (paperback)
Wisconsin Death Trip
0-394-73958-2 (paperback)

Susan Meiselas
Nicaragua
0-394-73931-0 (paperback)

National Archives Trust Fund Board
The American Image:
Photographs from the National Archives, 1860-1960
0-394-73815-2 (paperback)

Alan Newman
New England Reflections:
1882-1907, Photographs by the Howes Brothers
0-394-74912-X (paperback)

Claude Nori
French Photography: From Its Origins to the Present
0-394-73784-9 (paperback)

John Perkins with the American Museum of Natural History
To the Ends of the Earth:
Four Expeditions to the Arctic, the Congo, the Gobi, and Siberia
0-394-50900-5 (hardcover)

The Photographers' Gallery and Jonathan Bayer
Reading Photographs: Understanding the Aesthetics of Photography
0-394-73584-6 (paperback)

Robert Rauschenberg
Rauschenberg Photographer
0-394-52054-8 (hardcover)

Marc Riboud
Visions of China: Photographs by Marc Riboud, 1957-1980
0-394-74840-9 (paperback)

Jonathan Bayer was born in New York City in 1936. He holds a B.A. in architecture from Harvard and an M.A. in international relations from the University of Pennsylvania, where he taught political science for two years. During the 1960s he worked as a research journalist and editor in Washington, D.C.; since 1971 he has been a free-lance photographer in London. Mr. Bayer has exhibited at numerous galleries in New York, Washington, London, and Southampton, England. He is the author of "5," a photo essay, and "Photography and Perception" (*Artscribe* No. 7, London, 1977).

Ainslie Ellis was born in 1920. He has worked at The London Gallery, London's first gallery devoted to surrealistic art, at Joan Littlewood's Theatre Workshop, and for the BBC. A self-taught photographer, he ran his own studio, Studio B, from 1955 to 1960. Between 1961 and 1977 Mr. Ellis reviewed photographic exhibitions for the *British Journal of Photography* and conducted a series of interviews with prominent photographers for the journal. He has also contributed to *Creative Camera* and *Photography*. Mr. Ellis now runs his own one-man word-and-picture studio, Studio Y, in Brighton, England.

Born in 1942, Ian Jeffrey is an art historian who lectures on art history at the University of London. He is on the Art Panel of the Arts Council of Great Britain and organized for them "The Real Thing," a photographic exhibition mounted at the Hayward Gallery in 1974. He recently organized "City Scape," an exhibition on urban themes in British and American art from 1910 to 1940. Mr. Jeffrey also reviews for Studio International and the *London Magazine*.

Peter Turner studied photography at the Guildford School of Art in the late sixties. Since then he has worked as a free-lance photographer and at the magazine *Creative Camera*, where he is now co-editor. Mr. Turner is on the Photography Panel of the Arts Council of Great Britain and has organized two of their touring photographic exhibitions, "Singular Realities" and "Through Other Eyes," and one-man shows by Bill Brandt and Tony Ray-Jones.